W9-DJI-471

Balance Point

Poems by Ruth F. Eisenberg

ISBN: 0-931289-01-7
Library of Congress No.: 89-61672

copyright:
Ruth F. Eisenberg, 1989

artist:
Jedd Strange

editor:
Kathleen Iddings

SAN DIEGO POETS PRESS
P.O. Box 8630
La Jolla, CA 92038

ABOUT THE ARTIST:

Jedd Strange is a distinguished muralist. In addition to being well-noted for his paintings, he has received recognition for the originality of his drawings and illustrations which have complemented many book designs.

For Allen

Acknowledgements

*I would like to thank the editors of the following
publications in which these poems first appeared:*

ANDREW MOUNTAIN PRESS: "My Father Lived with Numbers"
BLUE UNICORN: "Pleasant Country" "Dispositions"
CENTRAL PARK: "Some Things You Can't Forget"
CROTON REVIEW: "Thesis"
EARTHWISE: "Depths"
FOOTWORK: "My Mother Whose Dreams I'll Never Know"
GREENFIELD REVIEW: "Oppositions"
IMAGES: "Partners" "Five Years" "Tomato Sestina"
NEGATIVE CAPABILITY: "Deflections"
NEW LAUREL REVIEW: "Ripeness Is All"
NIGHTSUN: "On Love and Matter"
POETS ON: "Salute"
POETIC JUSTICE: "My Grandson Reaches" "The Clearing"
THE POMEGRANATE SERIES: "Gift"
REBIRTH OF ARTEMIS: "Post Script"
WEST HILLS REVIEW: "Come Lovely and Soothing Death"

Table of Contents

The Face Under the Face

Margin For Error

WHERE SALT WATER MIXES WITH SWEET

Oppositions

To confront the darker side of light
is to illumine the shadow

is to ride the underside of a wave
into its curl and crash drawn upward

to focus on the tock in the stroke of time
the sound the clock returns

concentrate on the backs of fingers
the bulge of knuckles
knowing if the palm slaps
the force comes from the upper hand

Deflections

Safe on The Breaker's wall, we watch
waves rise fifteen feet
into the curl before they smash
against the rocks, fling spray twenty
thirty feet higher over our heads
brine salting our lips

     my father hurling accusations at my mother
     invective slamming our ears
     through an angle in the doorway I saw
     her rigid as a retaining wall
     bear the onslaught, parry the attack
     we tasted salt

If you kneel and peer
into still, clear pools
where salt water mixes with sweet
you will see new life forming

Hand Made

Mother was a hand
darting the needle through the sock
darning coarse stitches
back and forth to close the hole
strengthen the fabric

a hand to cup my chin
to dust the disappointment
from the furniture of my life
to catch my elbow after
it unwittingly slipped off a table

And I am a hand
in a world of words
that enter eyes, ears
Willed onto the page
pen gripped between my fingers
my hand is my mouth

Player Piano

From nowhere my father seizes my hand
making words run from my fingers
like the magic notes of our splendid Knabe
its keys depressing themselves as unseen
hands spilled Mozart into our living room
filling our ears with grace
notes and intricate chords until
the square perforations ran out
and we pushed rewind
for other unanticipated times
when impulse propelled us
to be in touch with creation

To Build

"I wasn't trying to shatter anything.
I only sought to build." Martha Graham

Take pieces at hand, some fiercely
refined, some raw as stone
and see if they will fit
where
and what recombining brings

all constructed on law
fixed but mutable
ancient but in flux as
the voice of growth

so towers peak
beyond the eye, trenches
reach genetic bedrock
and we all travel
through walls

Journey

Try me it said and like Alice she complied
and stepped into the alley where she'd never
before entered, the walls lit with posters
announcing other journeys with arrows pointing
in what seemed like a logical direction
How do you try an alleyway she said
although she was already far beyond
its entry *by simply using your eyes
as guides* and the walls glowed as though
in affirmation and she put one foot in front
of the other and clasped her hands behind
her back so nothing she owned
could stop the passage

I am afraid to go further she said
trust me it responded, not knowing why
she did the way was dark but suddenly
illumined by shafts of sunlight that caught
the mica into flashes and she saw a picture
of her mother in a pink blouse and pearls
(strange my mother didn't like pink
she thought) she passed beyond to more dimness

lit by blue neon tubes that made her shiver
because the light was cold and her skin turned
clammy but she felt forward was better
and hearing her heels click on
the barren floor she proceeded and forgot
to wonder where it would end

Have I gone far enough she asked
there was neither answer nor echo
the chamber too full of her own
silence yet from the silence she knew
she had an answer as surely as her father
clapping her on the shoulder when pleased
or giving her ten dollars so she advanced
although worried and began to sing
to comfort herself, come to me, bend to me
some day he'll come along, somewhere over
the rainbow, singing as though her life
depended on her voice and it did

She stepped with care and must have spoken
aloud *Is it worth it* because the walls heard
displaying bound volumes of early diaries
in leather and gold and a Star of David
gleaming softly its six points lit and spools

of film in cannisters on shelves
as though waiting for an edit she saw too
that nowhere were the walls blank but
a portrait gallery, some with small overhead
lamps, some canvasses so dark
she knew she'd need a flashlight

How will I know if I've gone far enough
the voice answered *you'll know* as though
that were a help and she began to feel a fool
lacking only cap and bells for having begun
when she arrived in a large room
with latticed windows each of which opened
to a different view *what am I to do here*
in answer a table appeared on it a pad
and next to it like Arthur's sword buried
in the boulder a pen to be drawn forth
and it said *take me*

Conundrum

And if I were to meet the dragon
to confront its snorting nostrils
and fiery tongues

and meet it alone
in a circular space with high walls
and no visible exit

Recognizing
that no weapon made by man
could pierce that armored heart

but I could find release
in its dying burst
its blood being my exculpation

what weapon could I
draw
for the necessary wounding

Double Vision

Dry
cracked
earth

dry
crusted
earth's skin
crumbles

in fingers
into dust

flies
from fingers
changes
earth's shape

Dry
cracked
earth

dry
crusted
earth's skin
crumbles

in fingers
into dust

flies
from fingers
changes
earth's shape

Depths

Pocked by rain drops
snapped twigs
bits of residue
stagnant
water too black
to see bottom
Yet far under
springs seep
unrevealed
except in winter
where rocks grow icicles

* * *

Solstice, moon phase
darkness of day
all measure winter
But what of those winters
when the mind a tundra
winds howl
sources stay frozen
and spring reveals
deeper, more solid ice   .

OUTSIDE THE GARDEN

Outside the Garden

For life is no Tivoli.
Only the young imagine it so:
a garden of candy-colored lights
grape and lemon flowers in trees,
where fountains bubble in clear tubes,
the sky filled with fireworks and fanfare.
In Tivoli, Columbine always wins her true love
and the Queen's guard marches to its own music.

But look again at mute Harlequin
whose guile conceals simplicity; check
the trapeze act performed with a safety net;
watch the teetering clown on the high wire
whose clumsiness mocks his practiced skill:
Hints of the world outside Tivoli's gates
where magic is not bought for a *kroner*
age not arrested by delight.

Thesis

What about Mrs. Noah? What about
the housekeeping on the Ark?
Who do you think fed the animals, cleaned
stalls and settled feuds and squalls?
Some of those pairs bred mighty fast
and only the cats cleaned up after themselves.
She had her own kids too, squabbling
with their wives, squabbling with each other.
And who do you think quieted Noah
when he had doubts? Talk of forty days
and forty nights. Sometimes Mrs. Noah thought
the drowned ones were lucky.
When the waters receded, the Ark
was a stinking wreck. Rations were short
and tempers shorter. Noah watched for the dove
while Mrs. Noah worried if they could hold out
before the cats ate the mice
and the elephants stomped everyone to death.

Typically, for piety, obedience and leadership
Noah gets all the credit.
At least Adam and Eve took the rap together.
But Mrs. Noah is our first neglected housewife.
Proves the Bible was written by a man.

Dispositions

We become disposers
of pots and pans, mementoes of Vienna
grandma's chair with the mended leg
We empty bureaus, find scattered
snap shots, saved thank you's
a yellowing lace hanky,
and in its gift box, even the ribbon saved
the daisy pin
when she turned seventy

We work alone
call auction houses, Goodwill
save what we can that fits
with our own households, steel
ourselves to toss away the cracked
Willowware, worn nightgowns and weep
unexpectedly over a blue blouse,
the one she wore her last birthday

We sweep the bared floor
walls echoing when the broom knocks
against the kitchen frame

Windows stripped, disconnected
telephone, room bereft
we close the front door
her voice still behind us

Post Script

You left so suddenly that day
dressed in light cotton
the couch held your impression
the telephone rang and rang
in the heavy air
light brightened and faded

After I hold my grandson
I look at snapshots of you with yours
ten years younger than I am now
I can cover your image with my thumb
but not lift your print off the page

You left me ignorant
took with you answers
to questions I had not yet figured to ask
Did my baby also butt his head
against your breastbone?
his small wet mouth try to eat your cheek?
Did you too smile all the way home?

Some Things You Can't Forget

(for Saul N.)

How tossing the baby in the air
for target practice
they filled it full of holes
flipped it back to the mother
How mocking they
ordered a line of march
not counting
on living witnesses

At our kitchen table you
pried your words, reluctant rocks
from a buried past
We studied our knuckles
heard the refrigerator stop humming
the dripping tap loud as a tattoo

Time's Tables

To get over a death
takes two years, my aunt said
Like everything true, it isn't
because like everything else that
you feel, time runs in different
zones and sometimes you
know you will never cross
the 180th meridian

Dreams are the best proof
They seize your sleep
into convulsive memory that leaves
you shaking like a child
Although your face has lines
enough so all the world knows
your age and two years is a drop
in life's cup, at the same time
it is an eternity that never passes

Farewell

Your collar grown too large
since the last time I slipped it on
In my hand you are too light
and limp, no feisty legs
pushing to get down

Little cat on this stainless steel table
listen to my voice as you leave
your life was often lonely
but free of fright
you slip away with help

I rub your fur
You stay warm under my hand

Come Lovely and Soothing Death *

Come to the hospice where hope is gone
to the cancer ward where bones break
and blood thins
and come soon
to scorched lands where bellies swell with air
and babies can no longer cry
Death, gather these babies
distended by pain
who will never know other than misery
Death, come to the incontinent
before all dignity is gone
Visit the house where the old sit
blank as walls
with tissue paper memories
where unrecognized sons and daughters weep
Come to those who neither live nor die

*From Whitman's poem: "When Lilacs Last In The Dooryard Bloomed."

Ripeness Is All

Even the furniture sweats.
Dogs pant dry tongues
while sidewalk kids hold spitting contests.
August droops through vacation
and campers stall the roads.

In Freeport
you whipped me with wild words
and spent, fell asleep.
I stood at the locked glass door
trapped on a tropic island
in a room cold without air conditioning.

Sand castles wash with the tide.
Peaches are rotting on trees.
Nights exhaust and
life collapses into fall.

San Juan, Dec. 31, 1986

"About suffering they were never wrong
the old masters: how well they understood
its human position: how it takes place
while someone else is eating or opening a window"

"Musee des Beaux Arts", Auden

The day of the fire
poinsettias bloomed in our hotel
the artificial waterfall rushed
tourists milled the desk fretful
for rooms that were still not ready

Smoke black and lethal
choked the Dupont stairwells
corridor walls smoldering
Chairs became cudgels to smash windows
others popped from heat
shards slashing the skin of sunbathers
Guests clambered over barbed wire

In the casino, against the odds
chips melted   Lungs afire
people perished under roulette wheels

Our room overlooked
the lagoon, fortaleza
I opened the balcony door
to a bright sky, waves
frothing against rocks
I smelled smoke, noted a plume
hovering helicopters
Changed clothes

Later, I thought of Breughel
and Auden

Guided Tour, The Colosseum

Nothing is as it was.
Walls of travertine stripped.
Absorbant sand that soaked the blood
gone. Skeletal relics of walls.
Trampled stones and bricks
mark the walkways, the shell.
Windows gap in blind gaze.
Still it looms.

Circling the pit,
we wander the inner ring
peer into cages for lions,
for people, low ceilinged,
closer to the arena floor.
Contestants, "We who are about to die..."
paraded through the Gate of Life.
Brave Caesar entered from underground.

We learn the categories of gladiators:
for life, for bounty or for honor --
the living pitted against ravenous hounds,
the dead so much meat.
Fifty thousand spectators relished the games.
With free lunch every Friday.

I begin to burn as the sun moves higher.
Here was Caesar's royal box.
Here the Vestal Virgins, above reproach
in purity,
gave the signal. Their thumbs down
spared the Emperor unpopular decisions.

2

Sixty years ago, Pope Pius purified
the place, consecrated a cross here
where the Vestal Virgins held sway.

I turn away from all who insist
that women must deny their capacity
to give birth -- to be holy.
Even as a child, I feared the aura
of a nun passing: white wimple,
rimless glasses, black beads
her rope of faith. I twisted a button
to ward her off.

Each Easter, the Pope returns here.
In unholy Rome, I have stepped over trash
in the Borghese Gardens, stepped back
from pissed on sidestreets near the Trevi Fountain,
but on this site
where entries to Life and Death
were set by roaring mobs,
the flick of a thumb —
a cross proclaims hell holy.

Rearrangements

On the day when all love will have gone
up into the burning that fuels the mushroom cloud
when the earth is bright cinder
and the all too solid flesh has melted
and no one will have survived strategy
or hate or love
neither the love one has
nor the love one has not
each broken down in the red smoke
blown into the cerulean
infinite sky that has absorbed
our finite speck, will we be one
with God and will He be able to forgive us
who forgot to lie down in green pastures
and instead vaporized the still waters

Driving in England

Along all roads
stone walls
shaping ways
inviting scrapes

Barriers enclose
sheep, cattle
prevent straying
out or in

Hadrian's wall stretched, it is said, from coast to coast now
crumbled, vandalized by centuries and farmers needing
the precise Roman stones used to wall out the Scots

                    So much for walls
                    the Great Wall
                    Berlin
                    What was it Frost
                    said about good
                    fences and good
                    neighbors

Coventry Cathedral

Nothing prepared us for it
Not the lookalike streets
traffic snorting and stopping
punks hanging outside pubs
pints in hand celebrating Sunday

Some people hate the structure
Even the guide books hedge

We climb a rise
note smooth red walls, tall slit windows
Saint Michael slaying the devil
A lady of good works selling raffles
Children in mummer's costumes
Nothing prepares you

For the lurch of heart:
the spurting tear
as we swallow whole
the skeletal shell
empty apse and altar
a charred wood cross
crudely tied

Two words on a wall
Father forgive

Nothing prepares us
The wall of light
clear etched glass
antic angels dancing and trumpeting
the glory of faith and the faithful

The effulgent flood
of stained glass, of gold light

At Chartres the eye is drawn up
through a far distant window
toward heaven

At Coventry heaven swathes earth
and we share the radiance
in this tabernacle
whose cement is love
whose foundation is forgiveness

ENIGMA VARIATIONS

A La Chekhov

The way it is would you pass me the sugar?
no, not what she said how she observes
everything like a novelist, her correct pearls
the way light falls on cobblestones
Is that milk or half and half? I don't know
how to makes her out especially when her mouth
pulls down at the corner there is an obliqueness
that makes me think boy, this coffee is hot
that the details are there to put you off
so many false clues to keep your interest up
to wonder what shade of blue really matters

Sounding

I have nothing more to say, she played
with the bracelet on her arms a fine chain
that slipped through her fingers   You
have nothing more to say? he cleared
his throat, stroked his chin, rubbing a rough spot
where he had not shaved closely and wished
they had not started this conversation
I have nothing more, I merely repeat
she placed her hands carefully on the table
splaying the fingers and began to pick
at a cuticle   He sagged in his seat

Her thin words a flume in the air
he wondered where she would dive
next and if his whole world would be upset
in her plunge

Enigma Variations

I'll never understand why
she rubbed the bowl of the spoon
removing the smudge left by the dishwasher
the very quality
she held the spoon up to the light
before aligning it·with the knife
that attracts you to someone
in the first place
she pulled the napkin through the ring
placed it beside the fork
lined it up with the wine glass
is exactly the quality
that later drives you nuts

* * *

She leaned across the table
the problem is
she traced a design on the glass top
that upside down made no more sense
than right side up a squiggle
that curved back on itself
that whatever we do
her finger stopped drawing and tapped
the table top but made no sound
against the clattering
and chatter, the busboy banging a tray

and the noontime traffic slamming
brakes, honking   the two of them
an island of harmony
as he sat forward watching her finger
and listening to her hesitation
will be merely relative
won't it

                    * * *

It's all Einstein's fault   If he hadn't
discovered relativity things would still add up
He rubbed his face to cover his impulse
to laugh and said instead   We all have doubts
and bad days   Already he needed another shave
This is more than a bad day   She squeezed
her fingers together
All the pieces of my life keep changing
their shape   Nothing fits in the frame
Why keep the frame then? his voice sounded
unexpectedly urgent
as his need to breathe, to touch her
Her answer muffled
as from the back of her mind
Without it, what else is there?

                    * * *

Seems like I can't sleep anymore she said
and blinked strained eyes as she worried
her hand across her forehead furrowed
as a field where a plow had run amok
What use does staying awake have?
he replied too reasonably
for someone who finds reason
in the middle of the night a beggar
appealing to a nudist colony
What am I
supposed to do? I won't
take pills, booze is fattening
I keep sweating even with air
conditioning, and he knew, of course, no
answer to that question
asked ever since worry replaced
whoring as the world's oldest profession

* * *

And if you could chuck it all
What if you could just take off, a Rabbit
Run she challenged wishing she could see
his face   Reluctant to let a fantasy go
he did not answer, merely grunted
to let her know he heard as she
continued   millions of people
have wished the same except
if you get to wherever
do you really think you are free
He adjusted the receiver on his shoulder
the telephone wire carried no impulse
her question vibrating

* * *

What are you afraid of? A zombie
coming out of the woodwork?
Don't be so smart he said you just never know
But why should that be reason to stop?
I hate change he said   What a waste
of energy she replied as the lights
dimmed then brightened
as though some Con Edison elf
chose to cast an editorial opinion

* * *

I want it over she said her jaw so set
he thought he could hear her teeth grind
It never seems to end
like the goddamned river you can't stem
the flow, her words bitten
each syllable spit upon the ground
He looked away, her anger not at him
saw the flotsam floating on the water
bits of plastic
I'd stem it for you if I could
he said flinging a rock
that sank with scarcely a splash

* * *

She pressed her palms together
looked at the steeple of her fingertips
I wish I could pray, her hands rubbed
each other without volition
Why can't you? his voice lifted in surprise
She would not meet his eyes instead
examined her fingernails as though searching
their hard, shaped surface

Because I don't believe in it
it's just another form of talking to yourself
I thought you said, his eyes on his fingers
picking at a slub in the silk rep of his tie
I thought you said you couldn't pray

* * *

When you leave shadows grow longer
and indeed light did seem to play
a disconcerting dance on the walls
the blinds controlling a pattern cast
by leaves blowing in the cold October wind
I know it's foolish to feel so
or say so but the absoluteness of complete
dark is somehow better than its advent
her voice soft, meditative touched his ear
an oboe playing in a low register

Circling

We wanted a fruit tree, planted a plum,
then a peach which grew one rotten fruit
before it too died. Resigned
we planted a maple so spindly
we could circle the tree
with our thumbs and middle fingers.
It bent with every wind
drew water from clay soil.

Winter-stripped the tree is fuller
than we ever thought it could be.
For many springs the seeds have flown
their green wings. The trunk now needs
both arms to circle it.

The maple casts the shade we wanted
on the house we left
when we knew
our arms could no longer
circle anything together.

To P.

You came to me in dreams before
you came to me
Gone you come to me still

I would still know you
were we to meet at a party
you'd never attend

You brought me to the headwaters
of the Mississippi but
it was October
and I could dip in only a toe

You never would let me see
the scar across your back

Arrive at my door
I doubt I would let you in

Available Light

You wonder about your eyes that failed
to signal, about that blindness
that made seeing impossible
down a platform of trust
whose edge you stepped off
with neither inquiry nor regret

You wonder about touch
that fine sense that should discern emery
from honesty even in the dark

What scents have escaped?
What sounds? I have heard
elephants communicate on frequencies
too low for human ears

What else travels on frequencies
too high, too low? dark
beyond our vision's comprehension
And what of the heart
whose failures must remain unrecorded
else the world's balance tip unalterably

Salute

Not for me
ice transforming
twigs and branches into glitter
or snow fluffed on bare hedges
decorating dark trees

I hail
the bare branch
the hard bark
of winter

Last Words

Then
the prophet said:
To the stars
we must return
that refuge
of surprise
for those who see
sky only
as blue or black
or blank
In the whirling
center of all matter
may be
all that matters
And we will not know
until that moment
beyond knowing

If you can't
fall heavenward
tie your last wish
to a comet's tail
Riding it
you will sweep beyond
your wildest prayer
to only
the Lord knows what

THE FACE UNDER THE FACE

To Light a Scene

Steady a cold beam. White light
sharpens features, each scar a seam.
Dim. Add pink to flush the cheek,
quiet the heart
and we restore lost youth.
Dim further
the nose casts its own line
but the eyes, the eyes
become tarns.

Lighting down, add a scrim.
Features blur, bodies bulk silhouette,
appear stage center as though
waking from a dream.
The scrim divides
applauding hands from fragile dream.
We touch a secret self.

Tomato Sestina

August again, the tomatoes are plump
and squirt with each bite.
In my kitchen, I measure redness
and think of Pop standing in the garden
with a salt shaker in one hand,
in the other, a tomato ready to split.

He needed no knife to split
that red skin. He would heft the plump
fruit with his hand,
polish it on his shirt, salt, then bite
and seeds would spurt all over the garden.
In a ripe tomato there is a redness

that nothing else can match. The redness
is not of the skin alone, for split
the fruit is just as red. In the garden
he grew beans too, and radishes, plump
as Christmas balls which he could not bite
when pulled. Instead, he'd hand

them to Mom to wash. She'd hand
them back, their dark redness
shining, stems and roots cut, and he would bite
into their white sharpness, his teeth splitting
each radish leaving a plump
half moon. Back he'd go to the garden

the 8 by 20 victory garden
in which with his suburban hand
he grew vegetables. Plump,
he'd bend over the weeds, redness
flooding his cheeks. We thought he'd split
his pants, but no. There was no bite

in him then, a joy of earth. No bite,
no malice. A business man in his garden
growing tomatoes 'til they all but split
their skins. He'd lift them with his hand
as they turned from green to pink to redness
that outshone the sunset. That red and so plump.

From such plump memories, I take nibbling bites —
in ripe redness the best of my garden
fondled with time's hand, whole memories not to be split.

Gift

"A violin was giving itself to someone."

Rilke

A violin was giving itself
to someone
but my lamp sings
only to me
Of ancient design
white china
A blue fluttering bird
beak open
sings near a blue
flowering tree

My mother stroked
the bird
into song
I hear
my mother's hand

My Mother Whose Dreams I'll Never Know

Every couple of years dad gave mom a juicer
chromed with a crank shaft, even an electric
but she'd go back to the green glass reamer
bought for a quarter at the Five and Ten
between the cosmetics and the depression glass,
and squeeze oranges by hand
fishing out pits with the point of a knife
and pour the delicious pulp into a glass.
Slender in her house dress, did she ever dream
of wearing gold lamé or tailored pin stripes?

When the grandchildren came, she'd line up
an army of oranges on the counter, orange balls
sweating small beads in the Florida morning.
As she cut them, they would rock
their sweet smell drawing us to breakfast.
In her bottom drawer, essence
of Chanel, Tabu.

In the dim kitchen, her hands knew
where everything was. The clearest light
came from the open refrigerator, beaming
until the door was slammed. She worked fast
chipping plates, dropping forks, everything
took too long. What was she hurrying to do?
Sunday mornings mounds of scrambled eggs, bacon
cream cheese with lox and bagels
tall cold glasses of milk...
My mother whose dreams I'll never know
drank her scalding coffee black.

Natalie

She lives by the river
and the river flows in her
in a fluency of eye
the deeper reaches of voice
flows in her poems in tides
and seasons
in her laugh, drawn
upward from riverbed

Flows in her daughters
each a vessel carrying gifts
of voice and language, dark beauties
who float on the river even
as they carry it within

In the play of pictures in her mind
she runs unexpected juxtapositions
long corridor of her eyes
song ripples as gold foil
She has written
that everything must leave its mark

. Water carves its own banks

Monet's Pond

All his life under the surface
I stare until a bubble
breaks the water from a fish
Light shimmers where tadpoles stir
their tails flicking stillness
broken with a croak
of an invisible frog

The longer I look the more I see
under the strokes
I am willing to wait for his dawn ·
his dusk to move
into my own discoveries

Reconciliation

God knows your demon has refused
to be exorcised
Pop, let me try again

        I don't want to think hospitals
        don't want to push wheelchairs
        in my brain — I try
        to invoke Macy Parade memories
        You breast-stroking in Rockaway waters
        quarters under saucers for my movies

        My daddy always
        had full pockets for me

I summon you dressed in a tux
Or returning from a fitting
four new suits
pin stripes, glen plaid —

        Hospital gown, IV
        surgical stocking
        one slipper under the bed

        Memory whirls
        a helix funneling
        to that one
        inexorable
        day

In bed, only one knee to bend
one leg to lift the sheet
You wave your hand
dismiss everyone
but me

Fix my stump, Ruthie
you charge
your eyes opaque
I do
my face marble

You send me off to lunch
I swallow my throat
step into an elevator
face tight as a plate

      Nothing else remains of that day
      Only that sentence

For your pride, delight
I passed Shakespeare with an A
made the Dean's List
earned a Masters
But you never told me
whether I flunked your test
or scored my highest mark

      My need is a clot
      Amputation stumps inside my head

When that door shut behind me
        Did you close your eyes
        run your fingers down your hip
        your thigh?
        Where along the bandages
        did they arrest

        Did you lie restive
        unable to reach down?

        Or slip into sleep
        grateful to be numbed
        from worry and pain?

        Is it possible
        that you never
        gave a single thought
        to what I can never forget?

Of one thing only am I certain
Had you been offered the choice
of life with one leg
or death with two —
You had what you wanted

                    * * *

My two legs kick across a pool
run errands and bend
when I need to stoop

My mind halts   My father
you were little older
than I am now
You tested me
but what did you face?

Didn't you know
no one could fix your stump

You limped thereafter
Yet I cannot believe
you intended to cripple me

Perhaps I have yet to learn
there never is
a single truth

Return to me whole
father I so loved
Let this be the last time
I pull the blanket back

Five Years

One orange and blue October day
I was wheeled into a sterilized room
saw only the ceiling
before everything disappeared.
Later I glimpsed a sliced piece
of unstained sky in recovery
and closed my eyes relieved
I would see it clear and cloud.

I had harbored a wild cell
anchored in my breast without my leave.
It gone, my flesh did not close seamless
but like the line between sky and sea
the slash remains
memory's chain.

Five years
stresses vulnerability,
each cyst a worry to be drained:
slab tables, technicians with machines
drop ceilings, their squares perforated
by symmetrical holes, the squeeze of mammography.

All deadlines met, countdown complete,
passing limitation is launch —
past cathedral ceilings, beyond Alpine peaks
toward the unknown
cruising at effortless speed out, out
in the limitless blue.

Resolve

Who are you? I ask my three year old grandson.
Somebody, he responds.

It took thirty-eight years before I could
reject all labels of definition
by which I spelled my obligation
to exist, thirty-eight years of Jew,
New Yorker, later wife, teacher
mother. That night
I looked into the mirror
and answered the question
with two pronouns
finally
I am I.

Weeks later, crossing the Whitestone Bridge
the kids asleep in the car
Easter Sunday behind us, I, exultant,
powered the car home.

The somebodies we are
the I's we must discover and re-
discover shout their claim
tonight as I battle
to keep myself intact.

I am I
tooth, nail and guts
for as long as time will let me be.

ReinCarnation

If I have to come back
let it be as a car, a Porsche
or a Rolls
one that is pampered, polished
with a soft chamois cloth
I want my nicks to be worries
winter hesitancies real cause
for concern My interior
vacuumed, immaculate
And when I'm taken on the road
pointed in the right direction
and given gas by a tender foot
all I'll have to do
is spin my wheels

MARGIN FOR ERROR

Intervals

When the trapeze artist lets go
sometimes her body turning
in a whirling somersault
            moving high above the net or
no net
toward another bar
swinging its own pendulum
beat
            how long is the interval
if she realizes the rhythm is off
the speed of her hurtling not quite timed
to the thrust of that slender bar so that maybe
she can
            and maybe she can't grasp it
And when she does,
            her arms extending
hands clasping using all her tensile strength
to carry her to safety,
her margin for error intact

is it any wonder
we gasp knowing tomorrow night
cannot be quite the same

Balancing Act

Sitting on a gas line with Henry James
or stirring soup as you finish a chapter —
some juggling is manageable.

But the high wire of several lives
in one requires more
than a book of directions on how to
climb a ladder bending like a thread
or tame a lion with a word and pen

The trick: to combine
"The Story of a Starry Night"
Tschaikovsky with an ASCAP beat

Fortunately, it's hard to burn soup
easy to wipe custard off your face
but tricky to dive into a ten foot tank

A different sort of plunge, poised words
plummet you into the unknown
It helps to know how
to tuck your head under
Only the clown knows
the face under his face

The Clearing

We walked guardedly, together
yet veering apart.
The glittering snow invited footfalls
but we kept crashing through.
Shadows from bare branches
made intricate trellises on the snow
a crisscrossed confusion.
In the bluewhite quiet, I began to shiver.
Your voice sounded steady, but I
was slipping, falling into coldness.
Your hand grabbed my arm.
Despite the whipping wind, I steadied.
In the cold our breath blended.
A goose honked, honked
until we began to laugh.

These are our own woods.
We can never go so far or so deep
as to be lost
except from each other.

SeeSaw

A seesaw is little more than a board
and a balance point
Riding it alone
you can only straddle the center
which means you never experience
its high and low reason for being

Love, my art teacher once said,
is when one long nose is attracted
to one short nose so the two
can rest in equilibrium

In Greek mythology the self
was double but got split
the rest of history recording
efforts to reunite the halves.

The question is whether each half
is a mirror image like the parentheses
or a contrast
the night of day, the exit of entrances

I am drawn to the seesaw as possibility
When weights are unequal
what fine adjustments become required
if one deliberately bangs
the low end jarring the spine
and bouncing the other, or both
use knees as springs the ride smooth
and fluid as a sluice
Every extended ride invites invention

On Love and Matter

The dictionary says matter is corporeal, occupies space, the material or substance of discourse. Spiritual love is not matter except in the corporeal thrust of sex or in the salient pen changing forever the virginal page.

Consider, however, love as cement poured over rough sometimes prepared ground, smoothed even and regular before its final hardening. Soft, you can carve initials in it. Hardened, you can choose chalk or indelible ink for the moment or forever.

Love fills cracks like putty, shapes itself to make a plastic binding. Like rubber it bends, turns corners, stretches over objections and returns for reshaping. Overextended love can snap but handled with respect is incredibly flexible.

Love is wood, sound to the knuckle. Fine grains deepen with care, grow more beautiful, can improve with age.

Thus love is matter, the subject of this discourse, written in indelible ink.

On Guard

With a fortress of love
no one can scale
a moat no invader can cross
I circle them

Their wet mouths eating my cheek
I'd battle Martian zombies
tackle a great white shark
Even handle a python
could they ask me

But when I eat their hands
their whole fist slippery in my mouth
and they laugh, droplets
from the purest artesian well
bubble between us

Pleasant Country

We have traveled far, love, so far
our backaches come in counterpoint.
This country is an English landscape, tidy
with trees concealing the horizon.
I prefer not to know where land ends.

Familiar terrain yet new,
comfortable as a shaded hammock
recognizable as strains from *Boheme*,
I'm certain we've crossed this way before
but look there's a new house on our street.

The weather is more moderate too.
Occasional storms blister
but with the calm, the sky becomes
a splendid blue, the grass deep
green of sodded lawns.

We've arrived in pleasant country, love,
not distinguished for architecture
lacking monuments and natural wonders,
easy to live in yet offering
the surprise of wild flowers.

Partners

(In memory of Raymond Henri)

We joined hands when we danced
the pavanne. Moved together
letting the slow, grave music
guide our steps.
Holding first one, then the other,
paced each measure, turned and shared

as in happier times we share
the beats of livelier dances.
Bowing to each other
we move, in harmony together
create the steps,
and arrange our own music,

tuned to one another's music
as well. Oh, we have shared
kicks, twists, the halting steps
that make us wonder whether any dance
will ever spring again. We pause together,
mark time, trusting one another

to revive the spirit, suggest other
tunes, other themes, to restart our music
in a new key. Together
we revolve the polished floor sharing
technique, suggesting variation, dancing
newly invented steps.

When we climb to a new level, step
by step, we turn to each other
to celebrate in dance,
circle arm in arm to that ancient music
traditionally shared
by friends rejoicing together.

Even parted, we remain together
pace ourselves as we step
into tomorrow ready to share
one with the others,
legato or con brio music,
our complicated, intricate dances.

With each other to share
lyrics, music, square and solo dances
together, we galop in step.

My Grandson Reaches

for the north and south
poles to balance
his precarious hike
across
the mile stretch of the broadloomed living room floor

Wide eyed
with his drunken lurch
unfazed
by sudden sit
downs

He's up again
Homo erectus
All grin
and toddle

on his way
to *sapiens*

My Father Lived With Numbers

The bottom of a five as round to him
as the curve of an apple
its sweet heft in the palm of his hand
my father tasted numbers
licked words to do them credit
Grey ledgers, thick unbending slabs
swung open to reveal the precise
green figures in credit-debit columns
His eye would blink the page
calculate the total

My father lived with numbers
green ink for loss or gain
His eights unwound with a flourish

In his pocket a small black book
stocks, bought, sold: sweet fractions of gain
zeros linked like men hugging shoulders
My father spent his day
his brain calculating, risking

Quarter capitalist
he lived for the market place
sought salvation in Torah
and a good credit rating

Grandmas

Some grandmas are cookie-givers
who store special treats for every occasion
and whip out a chocolate chip
snap, just like that

Some grandmas are scouts
who dull sharp knives
smooth out bumps in the rug
and keep the world safe

Most grandmas have laps
big enough for more than one
grandchild, a book and even a cat
They have very long arms for hugging
and mostly don't admit to backaches

I am a grandma who sits on the floor
piecing together complicated waffle blocks
to build wobbling towers
as often, plus one, as they are knocked down
A grandma who likes to look
my grandchildren straight in the eye

A Sense of Fitness

With a side trip
you put your life on hold,
I said, and she thought it a good line
to begin a poem. So here I sit on Market St.
under a full moon and the steeple
of Faneuil Hall (unless someone misled me)
and think of wills and death
with a sense it is highly inappropriate.

Not quite a vacation, tomorrow
I will attend meetings. Now with a full
wallet I can wander around and do much
as I please except my leg hurts and
my feet are taking on that museum quality,
so I'm on a bench facing the Bull Market
(not too appropriate a name these days)
thinking of providing for other people's futures
when I should be seeking a lobster —
except come to think of it
the cholesteral is highly inappropriate.

Approaching Sixty

Protected from smashing waves
I swim out near the breakwater
Here near the dividing point
between safe lagoon and wild Atlantic
I breathe deeply and easily
Combined strokes have brought me here
where I am alone
but all along the shore
are sunbathers and waders

I tread water
turn toes sunward and float
liking it here, enjoying my illusion
that the rocks are benign
that tides pull toward shore
that I control my strokes.